ART OF *NAVIGATION*

ANDREW JEFFERSON-MILES

ART OF *NAVIGATION*

PEEPAL TREE

First published in Great Britain in 2003
Peepal Tree Press Ltd
17 King's Avenue
Leeds LS6 1QS

ISBN 1 900715 41 4

Art of Navigation was first published in a limited edition in
1999, under the name of Andrew Bundy.

ACKNOWLEDGEMENTS

Acknowledgements are due to the editor of *Sheffield Thursday* magazine, *E. A. Markham*, Sheffield Hallam University Press, in whose publication Part III: *Malory*, (issue No.6); and to M.G. Vassanji, editor of *The Toronto Review* in which the title poem: *Art of Navigation* appears.

No single reference or poetry book can be cited as source or origin to the title poem. The knowledge base depends on cross-referencing the latter-day astronomical sciences — radio-altimeters that failed on the inaugural flights of the passenger aircraft, Concorde; hydrogen-gas weather balloons; the rose-coloured hydrogen-dense part of the sun called the chromosphere; the process of nuclear fusion completed there — with the historically earlier navigations based on compass, backstaff and tables of conversion. The reader might be aware of the politic, scientific and psychological background to Europe's overseas transactions between 1415 and 1615; in particular, the quest, by Renaissance navigators, for the fabled, unknown, southern or austral, continent.

Italicised words in the text serve a number of functions. They denote an envoi in the stanza, as, for instance, in strophé II **Lateener:** *You shoot a star/ to fix your position*. Italics give quotation, such as that from Psalm 42: *but your waves and breakers/ have swept over me/* made a true compass of my own heart (strophé II); or, in strophé VI, from The Book of Common Prayer, ***For all Sorts & Conditions of Men***. Italics also highlight words key to the sense of a line, as those in strophé V **The African Awe of Armament:** What is the explanation/ for Therese de Lisieux's/ *high* level of prayer/ when it is by *outward* momentum that we are absolved? Finally, *italics* denote languages other than English, such as the Latin motto (strophé IV) so frequently inscribed on the sundial: *nisi serenas/ horas non numero*; appearing a few lines earlier, also in italics, as, */I/ count only the shining hour.*

Part II, a sestina of sestinas (1+6 sestinas), parallels a sonnet of sonnets (1 + 14 sonnets). Part III appears with the original gloss.

I would like to thank the poets *Anne Stevenson* and *Pauline Stainer* for their sustained, personal encouragement since meeting me in 1994; *Lucy Hamilton* for a remarkable introduction to the title poem; and *Margaretta* and *Allan* for their support during the writing of the book.

CONTENTS

To Andrea Offner-Lowry, Beata-Krista Kopp and Jocelyn Almond

PREFACE TO
ART OF *NAVIGATION*

What basis for the writing; what in answer to?

1. In a general sense critical theory describes how we appropriate, for use in our own lives, the lives in the texts we read and have had read to us. More recondite, it is by entering questions about the sorts of text we hear, and the sorts of text we miss within the same *oeuvre*, that we begin to make statements on the contexts and conditions of audition. In subtle gist, literary theory is axiomatic: where a theory is forceful enough, there is, inevitably, a sense in which it consumes its texts and agendas. Conversely, a theory becomes classical when it is thought to have been understood, which is to say, it is left behind or constructively challenged: by doing what the theory prescribes, new writings consume the theory, making critical approaches from that angle fulfilled, already accomplished; the new works pre-empting the theory, making it redundant. Thus both literature and theory covet ground primed for annihilation: to gather critical mass, theory must impropriate more and more territory, until it either atomises the kinds of literature it seeks to describe, or is destroyed by the proliferation of the very thing it seeks to justify.

Art of Navigation

2. The fate of those individuals who inherit multiple cultural roots and who must live and re-create in a [Western] society marginalised against its own rich origins; such individuals find themselves tasked to re-vision a society which, despite its deeply seated refusal to regard itself beyond a single invariant code of identity, is instinct with variation or deep convolutions in experience. Specific navigations or intiatives in futurity are made towards awe. The poet-specialist of register embarks on an unfinished process of reimagining with the past or unfinished maintaining of futurity. Such acts or offices attract and amplify certain kinds of work. The deliberate act of re-visioning the multiple roots of inheritance allows the conscious individual to behave as if humanity were to continue an unfinished search for an undiscovered continent, and it is into such a register that the title-poem writes itself.

3.   At first sight *Art of Navigation* assumes a certain acquaintance with the scientific inventions which accommodated Europe's overseas transactions between 1420 and 1620. The mythological belief in the existence of the fabled southern continent, the *Terra Australis Incognita* [The Unfound Continent of the Austral or South] powered two centuries of strenuous and remarkable expansion; from the initiatives under the Portugese Prince Henry the Navigator in 1415, to those of Sir Walter Ralegh in the Guianas in 1615. The hard-headed makers of state had more mundane reasons for funding exploration and a new, exact, empiric science was brought up to meet the requirement of enlarging the Exchequer:[1] new ships designed to ride storm; methods of rigging for sailing into the wind [the triangular or lateen; a corruption of the word Latin, i.e. Mediterranean sail]; refining the astrolabe with the compass, backstaff and tables of conversion for estimating latitude; tables to correct variation between true north [latitudation in the earth's magnetic field] and fixed north [the compass' card calibrated at home]; the technical term of 'shooting a star' meaning to use a straight stick to sight the altitude of the Sun above the horizon at a fixed hour, usually noon, in order to guess, or by looking up charts of conversion, calculate the ship's latitude; and of this shooting of the Sun being better accomplished on landfall than on a wave-pitched ship [*Section III The Good Burgher*]; or how lacking the mathematical skill/ imagination to use tables of conversion correctly, the recourse of a skilled mariner was to 'sail latitudes' [*Section III The Good Burgher*] until celestial [night-sky] observation fixed his latitude, and then his heading east or west until he hit land. A more mercantile reference is to the sailor's 'rumblines', the stripes painted on the side of the ship

to show the weight of the cargo. This is connected to a reference to the anatomist's 'craie', used to highlight the various vessels and conduits in diagrams of the body. In this way, the poem sustains the contemporary parallels between the anatomist's exploration of the body with the cartographer's exploration of the world, as does the punning between coastal/costal in *III: The Good Burgher*, strophé 3. If the reader is aware that the first printed map did not appear until the *Imagines Coeli Meridionales* [Picture Meridionals or Constellations of the Heavens] by the artist Albrecht Duerer under the guidance of two astronomers in the Nuremberg woodcuts of 1516, then he will grasp the reference to the palimpsest-charts inked in sheep-skin [*Section III The Good Burgher*]; or that if the reader knew the print in question, he would be aware that the southern sky had been poorly charted and that although the south or austral sky is far more numerous in stars, it had at the time far fewer identified constellations – and hence mythological beings – than the borean hemisphere [*Section II Lateener*]. In an era which had no time-keepers of suffecient accuracy to calculate longitude, not only did every bearing have to be calculated according to lines of latitude, but the timepieces employed had to be turned every hour or half-hour, a hopeless undertaking during a voyage which might last anywhere between thirty and ninety days.

4. Now to the relatively large number of facts concerning the sundial. Knowing, for instance, that the single fixed pointer on the sundial is called a gnomon [Gr.gignoskein, to know; a discerner, interpreter or set-square calculator] whose shadow cast by the sun creeps around the dial as the day goes by, will make the title of *Section IV The Oblique of the Gnomon*, clear; or that with the division of the day into twenty-four equal hours in the Fifteenth century meant that, to be accurate, the edge of the gnomon had to be parallel to the earth's axis, which meant that it must point true north [or true south in the southern hemisphere] and that it must slope at an angle to the horizontal which is the same as the latitude of the place, hence the cosmic reflex of the two fishermen who close the section, one whose paddle inclines true north, the other whose net angles to the latitude of the place; that a shadow is cast under the oblique angle for part of the day and recast over the acute angle for the other part, is helped by remembering that the Saxons divided the day into four tides; of which we retain 'noontide' and 'eventide', that residue of naming, colouring the diction of 'tide' in the same section of the poem.

5. The remainder of the knowledge-base includes the contemporary sciences which have received and deepened these Renaissance inventions: radio-signal altimeters such as those which malfunctioned on the inaugural flights of Concorde, hydrogen-draft weather balloons, satellite navigation, solar physics – the Sun's different regions: its chromosphere or 'sphere of colour' which gives the pinkish tinge to the Sun during eclipses; the photosphere, or sphere of light, is the layer of the Sun which emits light in the visible part of the spectrum. It is covered with mottlings or granulations, probably produced by hot gases near the surface; then, the process of nuclear fusion inside the sun whereby two hydrogen nuclei co-vale to produce one nucleus of helium, the reaction liberating, among other wavelengths in the electro-magnetic band, heat and light in the visible portion of the spectrum. Helium heads the group of elements in the periodic table called rare-earth gases [*Section I Imagines Meridionales*] that number also neon, argon, krypton and xenon; the 'swift particles' of *Section IV* are neutrinos, super-fast nuclear charges created deep within the Sun which can be detected and which are the only direct evidence that radio-astronomical observers have about the conditions inside the Sun; finally, the knowledge-base includes optics – the use of specialised refractors/ prisms to exploit [polarize, refract, reflect] the wave properties of light and so turn up a more precise means of determining the fundamental units of time.

Formulations of Contemporary Poetic Imagination

6. That consideration of time has to do with tentatives at an appropriate framework for history. Such tentatives, however useful as technical instruments, are never definitive. They will eventually concede to my recognising that I am a hybrid and composite inheritance through which, if I am to enjoin and exercise the free and continuing anthology of myself, I must keep the past open and, in a way, unfixed, unconsolidated. Mine is an ongoing ouverture and entanglement with states of being and the composite imagination. Running alongside the formulation of the contemporary is the embodied concept of time or Being. Conceived in its most extreme possibility, state of Being *is time itself*, and not *in* time.[2] As I write this Preface I am also reading Heidegger's 1924 lecture *Der Begriff der Zeit* (The Concept of Time) and it is refreshing to see that he is happy to abandon the preoccupation with a registering of sense data when we attempt to describe internal time-sense; a preoccupation that can be said to have caused serious *ralentissement* in the development of all European philosophy since the Enlightenment. Instead Heidegger remembers Augustine's dialectic in the *Confessio*, Book XI in order to speak of our *incongeries* with time. It is a canny choice, partly because Heidegger is addressing a Theological Society (the Marburg Theological Society) and partly because the choice of Augustine so aptly amplifies the concept of the *affectionem manet* or finding of myself *disposed* (*affectionem*) as the thing which is a permanence, which stays (*manet*). Heidegger calls it, *Mein Mich-Befinden selbst*; so that when I measure time, the thing which I measure, is *my finding of myself disposed, Mein Mich-Befinden selbst*. The current and permanent measurement of my disposed self means that the acts of summoning or process of literary composition requires that I maintain myself alongside my past even as I am runnning ahead through new displacements in literature. This produces time in that it allows the significant past to be repeated and recreated in how it is lived. Such re-histories inhere experience with futurity or array for new composition. The concept of time can no longer be considered a measuring from the locus of a time present, but is manifestly a 'how' in the process of Being. On this procurement of a reconfigured clock St. Augustine has this to say: *"affectionem quam res praetereruntes in te faciunt, et cum illae praeterierint manet, ipsam metior praesentem, non ea quae praeterierunt ut fieret: ipsam metior, cum tempora metior."* Paraphrased: "the transitory things encountered bring you into a disposition which remains, while those things disappear. That disposition I measure as a *contemporary* (praesentem) existence, and not with the things that pass by in order that this disposition first arose. My very finding of myself *disposed*...is what I measure when I measure time."[3]

7. *New register of tempora* is scripted into the Anglican Order of Service in Archbishop Cranmer's *Book of Common Prayer*. The readings proper to each Sunday and Feast Day in the Church Calendar work backward into three distinct historic reckonings: the 'Proper' of the Mass begins with Collects paraphrased from the Latin by Cranmer in the 1549 Tudor directive; continues with an Epistle – Paul's letters to his brothers-in Christ; and concludes with the Gospels; parallel witness accounts of the life of Christ. Thus the worshipper becomes active *through* phenomena of futurity, *through the 'how' of being temporal*: he reaches backward, firstly via prayer, then via interpretation and finally via testament. It is with these informations that the poem makes a new formulation of the poetic imagination wherein the *I* of the poem takes its leisure, its *anima ludens,* revising its way through its own intuitive clues; for magnitised to the the poem-body – *corpus poesis* – is analogy to that new register of tempora found in the Anglican Order of Service: the *I* of the poem being also collect or *oratio ad collectam* [I speak a summary, and, I speak something destined for an 'assembly of people'];[4] becoming aware of its futurities in its sense of providence or permanence next to the body of the other.

The Critical Milieu

8. so directly at the heart of cultural politics. Literatures of the revisionary potential that express an inheritance of multiple cultures is an hereditary succession that precludes the conception of identity and a single invariant code or parochial reality. Parochial alignments or ubiquitous texts claiming a reality founded on a clearly-defined way of seeing men and women living form birth to death in a solid material world are attempts at consolidation or false closure. They defend-unto-death the permanent and lifeless enchantment with the adventures of the empirical ego. For the gifted writer, alive to the multitude of cultures that nature and re-nature him, his programme of writing becomes a resistance to false closure and consolidation; a resistance to the fallacy of homogeneity and culture. Such a writer will by instinct generate literatures that prove themselves cultural nova.

9. I have chosen to address the ramifiations of the writing chiefly through the title poem since this is the first section of the book the reader will encounter. The technical experiments completed in the succeeding sections follow from this. Imaginative literacy is one of related but unclarified phenomena, such as those that generate sustainable languages of the imagination. The philology of signs, the phenomenology of emblems are means of sustaining strength of feeling and reversibility with time which expresses itself with the character of memory.

University of North London
March, 1999.

Andrew Jefferson-Miles

Notes:*The Art of Navigation*

1 Baker, J.N.L., *A History of Geographical Discovery and Exploration*, Harrap, 1948 cited in Hale, John. R., *Age of Exploration*, Time-Life Books, 1966, pp.12-13. Europe was short of metal to make into coin. Existing mines and deposits [gold in Ireland, silver in

Germany] were either exhausted or unable to cope with demand. Without ample supply of coin, there could be no increase in commercial and financial transaction. If economic necessity could be incorporated into a cosmogony of *paradiso terrestre* and the Christianisation of all God's creatures, then all well and good, this would better oil the political engines and conceal the hidden agenda. Once sufficent precious metal and spices had been found and enough Europeans were stationed abroad to exploit mines, secure posts and protect trade routes, Renaissance governments lost interest in exploration. By 1602, Pero Fernandes de Queiros, looking for backing for an expedition into the Pacific could report of his reception at the Spanish court that "sufficient lands had been discovered for His Majesty and that what signified was to settle them....than go in search of those I said were new". Embodied in this fable are two frequented conflicts; patterns of tradition versus the trajectories of the imagination.

2   Heidegger, M., *Der Begriff der Zeit* (trans. *The Concept of Time*), lecture to the Marburg Theological Society, July 1924, pub. Max Niemeyer Verlag, Tuebingen, 1989. The Preface uses the bilingual edition trans. William McNeill, Blackwell, 1992: "Das Dasein, begriffen in seiner aussersten Seinmoeglichkeit, *ist die Zeit selbst,* nich *in* der Zeit....Im vorlaufen mich haltend bei meinem Vorbei habe ich Zeit....Zukuenftigsein gibt Zeit, bildet die Gegenwart aus und laesst die Vergangenheit im Wie ihres Gelebtseins wiederholen." pp. 13-14.

3   Augustine, *Confessio*, Bk. XI. Quoted ibid. pp. 6-6E.

4   Harrison D.E.W., *The Book of Common Prayer,* Anglican Heritage of Public Worship; Canterbury Press, London 1946, p98.

5   Phrase coined from Wilson Harris's "Literacy and the Imagination – a talk", in *The Literate Imagination,* Warwick University Caribbean Studies, 1989, p.27; and in *Selected Essays of Wilson Harris*, Introduced and edited by A.J.M. Bundy, London, Routledge, 1999. On the illiteracy of the imagination Harris writes, "We tend to read the world in a uniform kind of way, a uniform kind of narrative, uniform kind of frame. That kind of thing might very well be one of the consequences, one of the

deprivations we endure in the light of traditions which we have apparently lost. There are many levels of society in which it appears that people are quite competent – they read within a uniform kind of frame. But their imaginations may be illiterate. We have heard recently that President Regan is the best communicator of any President in the history of the United States. His statements are very clear and yet it does not take us long to recognise the psychological fallacies (actually William James's term was the 'psychologist's fallacy') which run through his so-called clarity. We have that kind of clarity – what I would call false clarity. There are many kinds of statements which are made apparently for the benefit of the masses. Regan... communicates with this kind of clarity embodied in the William Jamesian 'psychological fallacy'. So many things are eclipsed, so many things are lost sight of, and masses of people respond because the way he communicates allows him to operate within a certain kind of frame which seems to simplify everything and make it easy, so there is no difficulty in comprehending what is being said. But we are up against this matter of false clarity (1999: p. 77-78)."

PART ONE

ART OF *NAVIGATION*

I: IMAGINES MERIDIONALES

i

disbelief in the readings
of the radio-altimeter,
the integers of the pulse
raised digitally at the wrist

not a garden,
but the array of Paradis:

granulations
against the azure downdrop,
the airship-in-silks
over the zeppelinstrasse

fusions of hydrogen
afford updraft
for Apus the paradise bird;

our chromosphere,
one of pulchritude
for those regimens
of rare earth

high mountain passes
where Indian swifts overlap
to thicken flight

river-trees
in lacrimans
of the white egret

the pressures
of the unconsumated ocean
unsighting the eye of the angel-fish.

ii

Even recent maps abound with the inaccurate,
true sight, always marked with difficulty,

what use the anatomist's *craie*
if not to stripe rumblines
in the body;

what good the map
if not to map the mariner?

Windroses
intinct the ship's cloth
in eights-of-gusts

the quartz-compass opaques
with the heavy-deuterium

St. Elmo holds fire by starboard
to densify the photon-gram.

How set a mathematical-jewel
to the world's calibration
when Time makes confidential scripts
in the astrolabe;

my foes taunting me,
saying all the day to me,
Where is your God?

iii

He is among the lattices
in the planes of symmetry,
he feasts upon the kernel
as though upon
the sweetness of the almond

the reflect of his each point
would bring us, we had hoped,
to self-coincidence

refracted for,
in the Atlantic's triangular plane

in the ships' timbers
caulked with molasses

was the salve not sweet
with which we redressed
those woundings
host-on the swart sub-species
below the boards?

sub speciae aeternis
exploring only such places
as are believed to exist

continued our search,
our El Dorados

were Polarizers
in a Nicol prism:

no synchrony
but doubly refracted;

ordinary-humanity
deflected out of the way

but our own displacement,
an extraordinary ray
that found the Americas
we had not anticipated

the Thing we sought
remained Incognita,
an entire continent
gone adrift.

iv

To the man graced with flight
these are agonistes
which overbear wings

plumes electrophorese
with iridium,
the poet's stylus,
radioactive with words
of a certain critical mass

bending backward from the metal
the tiny jeweller's hammer.

II: LATEENER

i

You shoot a star
to fix your position

come ashore
from the wave-list vessel

do you not remember me
from the land of the Jordan

the formal recruitment
of the twelve
consolations?

How un-zodiaced is the austra-sky
of gods, heros, animals

just that brief eruption
at the southern-cross.

ii

Out of sight of land
we are at the mercy of our instruments

a Wesleyan wind
evangelises the open water

from trial & terror
come degrees of trim
to the spiritsail

beside her three deft laterals
the lateen ghosts a fourth

we rig as though shaping trapezoids
in the heights of Hermon

deep calls to deep,
the roar,
of waterfalls

the theory was there,
worked out
by astronomers ashore

hosts of manuals,
tables that convert
eucharist

or how
translate the angle
between Galilean *plombe*
and Pole Star.

iii

The magnitized north-pointing needle
is fixed to a card
of compass-points principal

but your waves and breakers
have swept over me
made of my own heart a true compass

what is sacrament
when Earth's field exerts
the uneven pull?

voyage by voyage
we plot *variation*

correct the pitch
between north that is fixed
and north that is true.

III THE GOOD BURGHER

i

at home
I left a wife comfortable

my pinnace is stored in pieces
to be assembled overseas

with new land reached,
the costal explorations require
the shallow-drafts –
gram-craft equipped
for going up-river

we sound with axes,
handicap the head-winds
with weights of lead,
confiscate the silver
of the paling foam,
grapnels to open the fogges
that we might see

the parrot has become
a most fit companion
for the tropic sun burnt
the memory of home.

ii

What is a little untidiness,
shags of fleece
on the sheep-skin chart?

we measure
by the wool's rate of growth

what else will keep time
when the clock is at sea

and the hourglass
forgets to be turned?

Sailed latitudes
against variation

went with multitude
until we reach a known house.

iii

Shot the Sun with a backstaff,
drank water that was yellow and stinking

no second fate
save the sunspot's black-upping
on the cheek

blackfly browse the skin,
multitudinous as the *tournesol's* seed

faithful in love
I am turning to the Sun
holding to a belief
at sea, as in love.

IV: THE OBLIQUE OF THE GNOMON
For Julia-Maria Schmenk.

i

one way is left to discover:
to lie inward and naked with you,
count only the shining hour

deep within the Sun
light-swift particles
reconstitute the kiss
for their outmost work

it is a voyage shadowed with plasmas—
of gem-corpuscles
pricked in the ruffle of the blood

to begin gently,
is it not
a light-bringer's motto:

nisi serenas
horas non numero

where all the shining hours
are *now*?

ii

our meal is communal,
providence keeps me
next to your body

always naked,
you feed slowly
as though sustaining shadow in the sundial

past noon,
the Sun reascends to the zenith

slips skin
into the integumented tide

the fishermen haul
in the warm-yellow water;

one man's paddle,
parallel to the Earth's axis;
another's scoop,
for the edge of the gnomon:

as though to rescue such motion
from the holdings of the mythological islands.

V: THE AFRICAN AWE OF ARMAMENT

i

a buffalo-soldier
walks in Africa

whatever the reasoning
behind the Benin's graphic carving –

the dreads that betray
the European's origin;
the weaved, weft wool of the hair
of one who spent close time
with the buffalo-god

the flares in the relief-field,
fanned-cool with the fletchings
of pressure turbines –

the visage the carver gives to him
is the mask of a man, concealed from himself.

By making a model of an object
you secure its glamour

the soldier, incandescent –
four-fifths relief
on the Benin bronze cresset –
titrates three gunrods of serum
for the cultural transfusions:

William Blake's *Europe*
supported by Africa and America.

ii

The courtiers in the rose garden
cultivate the demoiselle

her throat is as the mute swan's government;
unvoiced by the strange
the throb which interferes
the heart
in flight

the warm signet
of her new kiss
seals the garden
against the late-suit

an absolution
for the *hortus conclusus*.

What is the explanation
for Therese de Lisieux's
high level of prayer

when it is by *outward* movement that we are absolved,
across centuries?

Bring me to all skill in Making
and the diction of my true self
that I might exorcise the terrible magic
of departure.

VI: *FOR ALL SORTS & CONDITIONS OF MEN*

violence is done the old beliefs

those for whom this appeal is desired
become conscious of being under no law;
but under grace

we do not translate the foreign speech
but *paraphrase* its greatest truths;
among the birds of paradise
the toucan's tongue
is slightly roughened

by the former and the latter rain,
the seasonable and blessed change of weather,
the making of men to be of one mind in a house —
restoring Publick Peace at Home —
the late heavy and dreadful deliverance
from those sicknesses immune to science,
and by that place of apprehension

where the world and where the register take shape

PART TWO

SESTINA OF SESTINAS

FOREWORD TO 'SESTINA OF SESTINAS'

The sestina of sestinas (6 + 1 sestinas) is, as far as I am aware, my own invention. Its structural analogy is the sonnet of sonnets, a meta-verse of 14 + 1 sonnets. The sestina's six end-stop/end-line words create an unusual focus that alerted me, as I wrote, to the presence of tantalising clues as to the language in which to compose my own self-portraiture in the poetic imagination.

There is, at first sight, a sense of the attempt in differing yet contiguous traditions (Christian, quantum theory, Hellenic-Dionysian, Celt, native lore in Europe and in South America) to comprehend a sense of origin. But there is, in addition to these attempts, a synergistic intensity independent of received traditions. It is articulating in the sestina conceptions other than those of received traditions. There erupts in the poem an uncanny, animal presence, akin to the *endography* or eruption in the contemporary literary work of an ancient validating myth, legend or folk-tale. It is as if the ancient legend or validating myth borrowed one's contemporary piece as if that piece were a substantive host in which to hollow out a rgenerative place to recompose and re-read itself. In the literary sense, that *endography* co-exists with the expression of what the Anglo-Guyanese author Wilson Harris has independently called the 'cross-cultural' (*Selected Essays of Wilson Harris*, Routledge, 1999). In the psychological sense, the validating myth in a literary work corresponds to the expression of Jung's archetype and mythologem (*Collected Works of C.G. Jung*, vol 8, 'Structure and Dynamics of the Psyche', p. 111, para 392, p. 558, para 293, Routledge, 1963).

Although it is possible to identify a number of theoretical sources for the cross-cultural, one cannot, it seems to me, make any direct claims with the *endography*. One discovers it in retrospect, once the work is finished, laid aside, then read again some time later.

Substantiation is in retrospect, indirect, by intuitive induction. To hit upon an archetype is also to initiate potential framing in the world's unconscious. That there is such in-determinacy in identifying which intuitive sources borrow one's writing does, in part, prevent a lapsus of the writing into an absolute or determinist frame: that is to say, it prevents the writing, until it is complete, from seeking justification for itself in a known archetypal and ontological frame.

The length of the sestina of sestinas would be 6+1 stanzas. Only five appear here. I am leaving room for future accommodations.

SESTINA OF SESTINAS

I.

My mother's house shored God's *fosse*
shrugged-off the shamble of the green *hill*
struck the mark of Cain in the knoll's disabled *head*
then the salvation wind through a bluish *wood*
quick as the fox in the yearlings' *den*
burred the maw, uprooted the *vine.*

I cleared falsehood's rust from the rufous vine,
bared faith's fosse,
prolonged the seam to Wisdom's den,
put a palisade in the mount of knowledge, where my blood and
the green hill
raised a bold circuit from birth's base to the surrender of the holy head —
a tercet of skulls above the grimacing wood.

What was my track through the unconverted wood;
what had I followed down the branching vine?
It turned the flexible stem to a spear-tipped head —
that avert, that turning-aside from the fosse
(final stumble in the browned shade of the hill),
drew me from the den.

Like so much flea from so much fur, I quit the henging den
but stay connected to the knoll's umbillicus — bolt in the ferous wood
rust with iron. A human clay translates the bell-shaped hill,
follows the little foxes to the tinkling vine;
from the lynchet's low bank it litters culture's fosse
with the catchecism of dolmen, cromlech and the menhir's
henging head,

then capitulates, loses the head,
that the heart's slow vintage might ripen in love's den.
But he who slips through the night must disappear – to fosse –
until pulled pregnant as the sound-bow from the wood,
until the bones blanch from training the twice-born vine,
until he climbs the chalk-cut skull of the balding hill;

but Time, our wrinkled father, bald as the hill,
precedes us. Near the grape-skinned moon, his wrinkled head.
In the night's black savannah the fox quits the vine;
the tribe is calm tonight, and full the den,
full like musk in the bearded wood;
all is close and unexcavated, close as old iron in the fosse.

And I make to straight the limbs in the green hill, make to clear the
littered den
but put things off, and naked in the wood, becalm the head,
join Christ's conversion of the vine-Dionysos: bridge Death's fosse.

II.

In Iris' *fosse*,
Temperance and the intercallated year;
but tempering the pyre
inflamed my own culture, forced
the rain plus the sun to breed
the rainbow and cleave the grain:

the poem's cleft grain
by the culture's seeded fosse.
What I do most is husbandry; *breed*
the short sonnet of thirteen moons into the formal year
that that same force
which sprang from the pyre

then felt age come-on, picks up sticks, again to set the pyre.
The charcoal-burner turns its grain;
Memory explodes. You force
with language; course the fosse
with blood. In flames the phoenix year
dies down to breed.

The scorched promontory, whose grounds breed
ash and stone. Beside the burst pyre,
a calendar of tent flaps and printed wind, flip year
over haphazard year. I find myself grain-
side, improvising; widening the fosse
below the scarred camp, canalizing with greater force.

New gods force
themselves among us, breed
bold mathematics from the Pascaline fosse,
reserve quanta of things still coming-in, tax art's pyre,
drag the sky's grain
out of true and recalibrate the year:

so increase the lines of cantus! Each year
turns another page of oratorio, forces
the eye to centre its polished grain,
lifts Spirituals from the sacred score. What breed
of man am I to will so much, to rescue a scorched art from the pyre,
to set the charistic crown on the grateful king in the borrowed fosse?

The truth is nothing more:a breed of love, the year
emerging from the pyre; what force
I have left, again ripening, like grain in fallow.

III.

The saddle of the dromedary *hill*
waits regent, gifts and the mortary star.
A language old as tribes
gutters toward conversion.
St. Paul toils in the night's terrain
blazing the trail of a complex sign.

That blazing trail detonates the lineal sign
so that those who lean into the uncial hill
become primers, touchwood to the terrain.
History ignites, sparks shower from the axle tree, the star-
shaped urge as sudden as conversion,
like the pax Romana to the strafe of tribes.

Come the twilight and the hares' exode from the subterranean tribes.
They draw the lair's fetor. They scrape a sign
that darkens. Twilight is Conversion
where the dead gods put-out on the hill,
each corpse laid-out in five points, like the David Star,
so that the shrouded sun dips its knee, hurries from the terrain.

Art put me at a differing centre, at the terrain
of starting fresh. Because of it, my ancestry — *my tribes* —
increased their burden with me. Like a fate star
estamped on the forehead, I grow an extruding sign
(above the small well-tended field, even a hill
will seem a wilderness, abjected from conversion).

To unraked land, the rake of moving water brings conversion.
In the unclarified terrain
black barges of boor-water irrigate the dried hill,
its dome, a burial-heap of tribes
who proved congruent with history. And the cruciate sign
used beyond further use, raises the star.

That Refiner, that star,
diffracts. The conversion
of a radiant sign
to seven bands of colour reconsecrates terrain.
With penitent strokes - ash bans - whole tribes
might absorb a new spectrum in the History Hill

and hammering for conversion, the metallurgy of tribes
pit the   terrain, gouge a sign;
and in the hill's burst furnace, the flare of the unextinguished star.

IV.

But what if the marriage takes place only in the *head*
creating a perfect work but a ragged life,
escalating the conflict between perfection and wholeness,
like a feline turned feral then won back from the wild,
who never quite resettles with the household odour,
but loses his straight line, makes you his turning pole?

Become a way of life: the tall pavillion and tenting pole
that navigate the complexed globe. A decade ahead
of delivery the great work plants its odour.
Fate clarifies. You fret with life,
have much to say, but find yourself with little say, and wild
with speech, bludgeon language; shape for the image of wholeness.

I ran round the village in the wholeness
of summer, a boy at the winding pole,
the blue flail of morning wild
with the unaccomodated circumfero; my head
and heart and hand quick with life,
the day full-blown with odour.

The *flair* of odour
transmits though time to assert a pattern of wholeness.
Every honest life
has seemed as pitted as the vertical pole
notched for lightning. But where the bruised head
startles for recovery, poetry strays in from the wild-

erness, pointing with its alien snout; wild,
and reclaiming me; a poetry ripe with odour
enough, to ripen me; raising the skin from the head,
lifting the curtain of cheek on the wholeness
of its fleshen choir; the glossal pole
overbrimmed with life

and trust, that there will always be life
enough to have and to hold with; that what runs wild
to be claimed over and again, will endure; will tilt the axial pole
widdershins - like the Venus rotation, her odour
snagged in brine, her delivery a rhyme of wholeness
where the sea pounds his symphony in the shell, *la scala, skulle* - head.

Old Grim and his black dogs strip Life by the throat. You lust with the odour
and the Wild Hunt; for the sake of wholeness
copulate with the prey: heft of the killing pole; severence from the head.

V.

It is because of too many years in the disfigured *wood.*
The suffocated light and my musculate strength
contract their radian. Because the resonating field
did not shut its pyrogenic lens
I am able still to re-cognate the world
from the unforgiving blaze.

Art is the un-flammable thing. Loss, that unquenchable blaze,
gut the cargoed wood.
The cargo-fox hoists his stink while we the world
reel and roar for strength;
but how live within the unshuttered lens;
how clarify the fringing liminal, the crossing-over field?

Transom Field
I hedge with loss. I blaze.
On Abraham and his ample bosom I fix a tightening lens.
Generations without number draw spoor in the misbegotten wood;
and I am here with them, my pride and strength
among lions, whom like myself, paw with the world

that just a single figure, living in a single-figure world
would dream the royal man emerging from the field.
He drips with dung, a god of soft ooze, his strength
and crown sloughed off, the skin a blaze
of sore: leper beside the disfiguring wood.
On him the sun will frank its cryptogram, widen the lens.

Art does its healing under the lazarine lens.
progress thrusts its cleft further in the world.
Divided, atomized, the rout of wood
disbands itself by a field
black with cloud come out of the north; the blaze
whitish from the high ground: presage of hail.

                              A man loses strength,
hails the dead below the blistering.
What can the body in a heap of blaze
do further with the world?
It magnifies its cry in the open field
Akeldama, where the flesh takes flame from blood-wood.

what, then, if I kilter for strength in that same deep world,
and though the view be occluded in love's lenses, the heart's field-
lines fluoresce, as do the polar lights above the ever green wood?

PART THREE

MALORY

INTRODUCTION TO THE POEM 'MALORY'

There is a well-known apocrypha of Beethoven's page-turner. It concerns the premiere of the piano concerto No. 3 in C minor, Opus 37, in 1803, at the Theater an der Wein. Obliged by convention to play from score, the great composer sits before the open page and begins. From time to time he would nod his head vigorously, and Ignaz Ritter von Seyfried would turn the page. The concerto ends in a tremendum: thunderous chords are embraced by enthusiastic applause. Von Seyfried stands back, looking well pleased to have followed it all, but later, many years later, confesses, of course, that nothing had been written down.[1]

To the casual reader, the intoxicating diversity in the world of letters implies a similar absence of 'notation', a similar *foglio in bianco* on which the poet tries out his inventions, and extemporises as he goes along. Continuity, knowledge, repeatable exactness, appear to be secondary priorities to the creative stream. But,

"The unfinished genesis of the imagination" (Wilson Harris)

"The material (world) united by the imaginal (W.B. Yeats)

"The mainstays of the cultural imagination" (Frank Kermode)

"The living mathematics of poetic knowledge" (Yeats again)

suggest something more prevailing, more effective that fleeting inspiration. These four formulations include the continuing role of Celtism in structuring European letters. That sparkling ribbon of trade, commerce, folklore, legend and mythos that historically ties Galicia in Atlantic Spain, with Brittany, Cornwall and Ireland, continues to exercise the fiercest grip on the great poetic imaginations:so that a middle European such as Wagner could locate as Germanic an opera as *Parsifal* at Monsalvat [Mount Salvation] in the

51

Pyrenees. His lieux for *Tristan und Isolde*, a legend with many Teuton variants, is that early shuttle service between Brittany and Cornwall. Tristian's night-sea journey furrows the love philtre (drug) of Celtic waters, his lips imbibing for all future voyager-lovers. Dublin Joyce likewise cites one of *Finn's* antecedents in Brittany: "Sir Tristram, violer d'amores, fr'over the short sea [the Channel] had passencore rearrived from North Armorica [Armorican Brittany] on this side the scraggy isthmus of Europe Minor [Great Britain] to wielderfight his penisolate war [Cornwall, the peninsula]."

Cornwall is the resting place of Joseph of Arimathea. The man who gave up his tomb so that Christ's body could be buried [John 19:38-42] lives, according to legend, a further four hundred years as guardian of the Grail chalice (the cup that catches the blood from Christ's pierced side). Once he relinquishes guardianship of the Holy of Holies (*Sanctus Sanctorum*) he becomes a tin-merchant out of St. Just-in-Rosewood, on the south coast of Cornwall, from where he trades across the Channel and round to the Mediterranean. Here the great christianizations of the C5 AD fuse with the anamnesis of Druidic traditions. The Celt arch-priests, erased from history at the Battle of Anglesey in 61 AD, enter myth, to later fuse with newer priests – the Christian Church Fathers. Ecclesiastical history compounds with pagan mythos, they power-up and send out radians that will reach the Middle Ages. Northside, on the Cornish peninsula, near St. Ives, is the castle of Tintagel. Reputedly an early site of the Grail castle [the wasteland] it had been, according to Geoffrey of Monmouth, a stronghold taken by Uther Pendragon with the help of the enchanter, Myrddin (Merlin). Here the legendary king of the C6 round table is conceived. Guinevere, Arthur's Welsh queen, brings as dowry, the round table; wooden and large enough to seat 150 knights (**Malory** in 1469-70, rounding-off ten years in gaol, and translating French Celtic sources:the C13 tradition of Robert de Boron and the Prose Lancelot).

Since Yeats, Joyce, MacDiarmid and Eliot, the works of David Jones and contemporaries such as Geoffrey Hill are evidence that poets continue to raise ravens from the Celtic wellsprings of the cultural imagination. The works come to be evaluated in terms of how successfully the author creates a new milieu with his material. How successfully do the the contemporary figures cover over the silhouettes left by legend? How fully do the contemporary figures inhabit the different levels of experience opened by the poem and its theme? Where the reformulation is successful, where literature realises its natural extension into anthropology, ethnology and mythology, it releases a freedom of the imagination, moves us profoundly, and invites to become its participants.

Notes

1. "He [Beethoven] invited me to turn over for him during the performance of his concerto movements, but – heaven help us! – that was easier said than done. I saw almost completely blank pages; at most, on one side of the page or the other, there were what looked like a few Egyptian hieroglyphics which served to remind him of salient ideas, but which were completely incomprehensible to me. In fact he played the whole solo part almost entirely from memory because, as was generally the case, he had too little time to get it all down on paper." The account, given by Ignaz Ritter von Seyfried, was published in 1833, thirty years after the concert, in the periodical "Caecilia".

MALORY
a narrative chapter

I.

At some stations no one got on,
being Sunday, and the people in the sacred hour
of meat, dark wine and the tyranny of the family.

His own sheltered a hundred wastes away
where no winds descend. It was his wife's body
now that carried his bag of scents:an aoelus

of fate, promise, and the kind of devotion
that touched. How simplified it seemed,
but something other was.

Already in the wood, a bulk snagged branches,
broke off short gusts, itched him like a hair-shirt
he dared not itch lest he betray himself.

Myrddin pointed out of the blotched window
"The mills," he levied to the lup-lup of the railtrack,
                              "once bled the region".

She is attentive, through duty, but mute with omission,
She coaxed a ligament to them –
an arthritis of habit bunched and inflamed.

"To forsake our track and cast due east across the slope,
the flight from flesh and rheum is a Lenten process.
Who can lay a straight path, when the plough lags in its groove?

Affinity is what we labour for; no longer glad,
but returning to what we most simply do".
Then the train whispering "destination",

low isobars accompanying the rut of the brake
the motion of air over the flat forms
the doors' decompression;

as sudden as unclasping a piece of intimate clothing
heat swells in the carriage. They step down
four hundred years, to the striae left by the Reformation,

veer off the main street,
entwine their limbs in turning
beside the torsions of thatched shack

hear intonings from within the occult walls
as though Taverner himself modes his Masses black,
past the "settings" of topiaries

that translate their bursts into metrical verse,
then the head-count of the cemetery —
the contestation of souls in the gravestone abaci.

They hide their shadow
in the slump of the church's porch.
Roses were engraved below the architrave.

To himself, "Are these sprays not my dreams snarled
in the copestone?" But she has pressed her bladed frame
flatter to him: "Let us cut through".

What is the cost of compliance?
What the cost of the persistant knot,
like a tendon he could not quite press out?

How it spirals into cramp! - in waves which take him
as far as where Sol beats the coppered drum of a lake,
round whose rim the silver and the birch

are bleached bloodless as Gwendolyna's thigh.
Oarblades splice the water in a darkening crop,
and Gwendolyna's arms are atremblin'

as they paddle the fluency of the boat.
Her nares flare. Her thoughts abort
against the steel of her lips

so that Myrrdin must look-up:
the brake releases a white hart
dimpled in the axle.

II.

Like a road run home to my own country
the epic opens a verse of exile.
The necessary stand back of distance

adjusts the tableau and the man.
We see a traveller rubid with storm
as though back at the Nile mouth

from which he starts his cheirographum:
handwriting things that enable us.
What growns into emblems pulls us with itself

so that we find ourselves crafting unexpected scenes,
as though from distant novae
we were to capture the Earth's own small information-star.

On its own terms,
art grows into the recondite space
where there will never and nowhere be

any rest. Always this, the road to my country:
one generation among the thousands of lifetimes
pushing the branch forever out on the world tree,

ripening within, though not knowing a great deal.
Buoyed to an ambivalent agenda
Myrddin and Gwendolyna at tow in the grey of the lake.

They stir a concentrix with the oar,
open a lens in the water,
unshutter the widening eye of a fluid camera.

Each stroke is a blur
and the font of the oarlock an unholy scrape
of bitters and grit to the touch,

the pulse drumming, drumming.
"Look Gwendolyna, look".
                              "No Myrddin, no.
It is you who looks and no longer finds us lovely."

A notched area is between them
A thing unknown, a slender boned artifact
skewers them as the point skewers its colon.

Whole aspects of the love-art remain unknown,
objects perish, as though with our own hands
we would press

for a fullness of image
behind the closing dial of the iris:
in that recondite space, reach for love's ephemera.

"If your arms are my prison,
I am a lifer in your embrace
which open liberated movement is no more a beacon

of welcome, but fends off: a gesture of alarm"
(her words darting like fry in the ambuscados of reed).
Somebody had dropped a pebble in the pan;

alone as a pharos, it glinted hazard.
Gwendolyna has stripped her skins of wrath
round the lair of hull, and lizard-like filtered into the lake

to circle the cockle,
her bikini flashing silver as a shark's fin,
the eye curved like knives to the sheltering prey:

no single composition would call
for all the instruments assembled in her,
each with its tonal speciality;

then the water streaming like rays from a mantle,
her limbs extend as though in prayer,
they flex like a bow over the tension of the bow.

"Look at the veil that you are wearing.
Your hair trails a mantilla of wetness.
Is it you whom I hardly know?"

III.

The heronic sun plunged its bill obliquely in the water.
Light was a startled shoal in the lake's dark humour.
Gwendolyna's exit is a porpoiseful arch

that subsides, froth-like, in the shimmer of the boat.
A thing will founder in perpetual error,
but one brave advance, sudden as rain

in the open, can change forever the love-experience.
Myrddin advances his craft to the shore,
flexes further the greening willow of the oar

winds whittle the pliant osier,
the spray specks the *canoua*.
Again the heron dips his ageing flame

to renewable baptism. Light let fall
an aureate curtain on the closing act of day.
Then rain like coinage

tossed a hard currency at the intimate fold of their embrace.
"What do you know of this work?",
her kisses, two by two, in the brown ark of his back.

"One pair of arms, one pair of lips
but of its kind, the heart is unique."
Myrddin throws in the stumps of oar, runs the boat in single file

to the meadowbank; knows he will not turn to her.
Already people are ceding ground. They quit the day park's
                                        good intent.
Solely nightfall shelters in the muscular rain

enveloped in its coelum; the intracardial space
between the fluid rods drilling, drilling.
First Myrddin, then Gwendolyn ascend the trace of broken
                                        floral trumpets,

the valves wet, overburdened; the ensemble involuntary.
"The heart is a hollow muscle. It functions only when engorged.
Only when engorged does the unchambered music start."